# HANDMADE
# Leather Bags
## & Accessories

**Elean "Birdy Teacher" Ho**

Design Originals

an Imprint of Fox Chapel Publishing
www.d-originals.com

Birdy Teacher's Leather projects (小鳥老師的春豬革鞄製作所：28款手創皮件快樂登場！)
by Ho Yi Lun
Copyright © 2011 by SYSTEX CORPORATION
All rights reserved.
English translation copyright © 2013 New Design Originals Corporation, an imprint of Fox Chapel Publishing, Inc.
Published by arrangement with SYSTEX CORPORATION through LEE's Literary Agency, Taiwan

Credits for the Chinese Edition
Publisher: Frank Lin
Head publisher: Green Su
Editor-in-chief: Carol Yeh
Photographer: Hally Chen

Credits for the English Edition
Publisher: Carole Giagnocavo
Acquisition Editor: Peg Couch
Editor: Colleen Dorsey
Designer: Ashley Millhouse

ISBN 978-1-57421-716-2

*Handmade Leather Bags & Accessories* is an unabridged translation of the original Chinese language book, with new content. This version published by New Design Originals Corporation, an imprint of Fox Chapel Publishing Company, Inc., East Petersburg, PA.

Library of Congress Cataloging-in-Publication Data

Ho, Elean.
  [Xiao niao lao shi de Chun zhu ge pao zhi zuo suo. English]
  Handmade leather bags & accessories / Elean Ho.
     pages cm
  Includes index.
  Summary: "Learn the art of creating elegant accessories from genuine leather with this inspiring guide. Handmade Leather Bags & Accessories shows how to make classic handbags and accessories with a decidedly modern flair. Gifted fashion designer Ho Yi Lun shares 28 simple strategies for enhancing any wardrobe with high-end luxuries without the high-end price tag. Even novice leatherworkers will be surprised at how much fun it is to make durable and sophisticated bags using these basic techniques. Gorgeous photographs, step-by-step diagrams, and easy-to-follow instructions make it easy. Readers can create a chic purse or shoulder bag to go with every outfit, and will find fresh and fabulous ideas for satchels, hobos, messenger bags and totes. The author shows how to make chic and urbane accessories for every taste, including iPad holders, business card cases, coasters, key ring tabs and much more"-- Provided by publisher.
  ISBN 978-1-57421-716-2 (pbk.)
  1.  Handbags. 2.  Leatherwork.  I. Title. II. Title: Handmade leather bags and accessories.
  TT667.H67613 2013
  685'.5--dc23
                              2013019322

Printed in China
First printing

# Preface

*Handmade Leather Bags & Accessories* is the creative effort of a single Taiwanese leather designer, Elean "Birdy Teacher" Ho, whose creative and academic credentials shine through in the high quality and beautiful craftsmanship of her work. She may not be a well-known name in the United States, but that is the benefit of introducing translated titles: they allow access to a whole new community of talented, inspirational artisans. When an English-speaking leather worker reads about Birdy's bags and tries his or her hand at making one, language becomes unimportant, and the human connection created by crafting becomes tangible.

Birdy's bags are not only spectacular examples of leather craftsmanship; they also tell a very personal narrative about her life as an artist. Many of the bags featured in this book were made for special people in Birdy's life, and many bags represent different learning stages in her growth as a crafter. This, too, enables the human connection that easily crosses cultural lines. Craft and connection: the two are inextricable.

We're looking forward to providing many opportunities for such connections by translating and publishing several East Asian craft books per year. These books have developed a passionate following despite being hard to find and read. As the books are occasionally found for sale on Etsy.com or selected projects are featured on popular English-language blogs, we know we aren't alone in our fascination. For a variety of business and cultural reasons, securing the rights and translating these books is a tricky proposition, and for that reason, most remain unavailable in the English language. Fortunately, after several trips overseas to appreciate the culture and make friends, we are confident that we will be able to bring many interesting East Asian craft books into English language publication. We love these books, and we hope you will, too.

Please feel free to write us with suggestions for East Asian craft titles you would like to see made available in English.

**Check out a video of the author teaching 13 essential leatherworking techniques on YouTube!**

*Carole*

**Carole Giagnocavo**
Publisher
Design Originals
carole@d-originals.com

# Table of Contents

# How to Make the Bags

81

72

8

88

87

72

97

86

# About the Author

Early on in Elean "Birdy Teacher" Ho's education, she learned about metalworking, woodworking, and ceramics, and she was convinced that handcrafting was bound to be an important part of her life. When she decided to study at Bunka Fashion College in Japan, leaving her native Taiwan, she paid her way by hosting craft classes in fast food restaurants, teaching wool and felt crafts out of a small suitcase.

She chose to study leatherworking at Bunka because leather adds an interesting texture to projects and works for both rough styles as well as for elegant styles. In her first year at Bunka, she took courses in making shoes, hats, and bags. When the time came to decide on a major, it was difficult for her to choose between shoes and bags. But, considering that shoes require sizing, she finally decided to major in bag design, which allowed her more creative freedom. For Birdy, creativity is very important—she wants every bag to be unique, and that's why her bag projects are always astonishing and beautiful.

Birdy's bags and other leather creations mix whimsicality and practicality not only in their design, construction, materials, and decoration, but also in the interesting, personal stories she has to tell behind each and every piece. If you read through the gallery of her work, you won't just be inspired to make amazing leather creations yourself—you'll feel connected to Birdy through her stories.

Through her three years of professional study in leather design in both Taiwan and Japan, Birdy transformed from a wool and felt craftswoman into a talented leather design teacher who now has her very own design studio called Spring Pig Studios. Now that she is well known and has many fans, her teaching schedule is always full, and she continues to craft creative and inspiring bags and leather items every day.

Check out Birdy's blogs to see more of her work:
*http://harui-harui.blogspot.com*
*http://yilun-ho-bird1234.blogspot.com*

## Exhibitions and Awards:
- Taiwan Designers' Week 2011, 3X3 Design Show
- 3rd place in the 6th Portable Bag design contest
- The Taipei International Arts Village, free art exhibition
- Tokyo, Japan, "The third floor in the afternoon" solo exhibition

## Experiences:
- Fu-Hsin Trade and Arts School, Department of Advertisement Design
- National Taiwan University of Arts, Department of Technological Design
- Bunka Fashion College, Bag Design

## Achievements:
- National Taiwan University of Arts, hand-made leather bag design lecturer
- Museum of Contemporary Art Taipei (MOCA), leather lecturer
- Xue Xue Institute, creative leather craft workshop lecturer
- Wen Hua University, handmade bag design lecturer

# A Few Words from Birdy (Elean Ho)

I'd like to thank everyone for your efforts in helping me prepare over the course of the year for the successful release of this book.

Firstly, I'd like to thank Lina for writing to me during my studies in Japan, cordially inviting me to write this book. I am deeply touched that you gave me this opportunity and at how you visited me again and again, rain or shine, at Spring Pig Studios to support me during my work. You also put my mind at ease by introducing the exquisite photographer, Hally, who took responsibility for all the photography of my work.

I'd like to thank my father and mother for their continuous support for their daughter through all my strange ideas, when I ruined my clothes making leather, and for putting up with my hard-headedness.

I'd also like to thank Mr. Zebra, who brought dinner to my studio after work and stayed with me till my work was done.

I'd like to thank my dear assistant Jo for coming to the studio so early every weekend and for sharing eight months of eight way dumplings with me.

I'd like to thank my friends (Old Chen, sister Tang, Xiao Xuan, Chen Wei, and others), because although I never had time to get together with you, you would all buy dinner and come to my studio to eat with me. We'd talk and eat and you'd even help me with my work.

Thank you May and Kitty for coming to my studio every Friday afternoon bringing with you your laughter and helping hands.

Thank you Liu San, Professor Ni, Serena, and Stone. Even though we haven't known each other long, I learned from you just how important dreams and reality really are, and thank you all for very kindly sharing your precious suggestions with me.

I'd like to thank my students for telling me countless stories about bags; your stories made making bags all the more enjoyable.

I'd like to thank the supply storeowners for kindly introducing all the latest gadgets to me, helping me to increase my knowledge and patience, and for giving me a discount on my purchases.

Finally, I'd like to thank my Japanese teachers of cultural fashion, JuChi MingZi and QingMu Kejiang, for carefully and attentively teaching me, a foreigner, for such an extended period of time. You made me fall in love with leather.

From the proposal to the creation to the submission of the draft, it took an entire year to prepare this book. During this time I never visited blogs, read books, or went shopping for samples because I was worried that during the process I would unconsciously mix in shadows of other artist's styles into my work. I used my own language to introduce the materials and tools needed as well as pass on all of the techniques I acquired while I was in Taiwan and Japan. In this book you will be able clearly understand the steps on how to create leather crafts and fully recognize that at times what you can't see is actually the most complicated!

# Tools You'll Need

1. Punches
2. Leather adhesive
3. Leather prep
4. Hole punch sleeve
5. Leather dye
6. Mink oil
7. Cloth twine
8. Plastic edge smoother
9. Hemp twine
10. Hollow punch set
11. Design chisels
12. Leather twine
13. Wax
14. Leather peeler
15. Stitch groover
16. Sawtooth awl
17. Wooden mallet
18. Ruler
19. Planer tool
20. Lighter

**21.** Flathead chisel

**22.** Plastic work board

**23.** Double-sided tape

**24.** Leather eraser (for pilled leather)

**25.** Leather eraser (for normal leather)

**26.** Needles

**27.** Button hole awls

**28.** Pencil

**29.** Pen

**30.** Wooden edge smoother

**31.** Clips

**32.** Branding tools

**33.** Multi-purpose snap rivet setter base

**34.** Tragacanth gum

# Gallery of Projects

Despite the dark circles and bags, Birdy's eyes still have the sparkle of a dream chaser! The following 28 pieces are the fruit of Birdy's hard work over the course of a year. Enjoy!

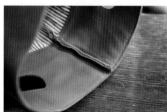

*Bag* 1

# Polka-Dot Clutch

Instructions p. 70

One Saturday afternoon in 2011, while I was cutting out circles from a sheet of blue leather, I noticed that the leftover sheet of leather looked much more interesting than the circles themselves! So I cut out a few grey leather circles and sewed them to the back of the sheet of blue leather, and I stitched a curvy swirl on one of the circles. It reminded me of the time my teacher in Japan had us practice stitching curvy lines, and how it felt like steering a car down a windy road. If you have the chance, I highly recommend you try it!

The orange leather I used is one of the treasures Mr. Zebra and I brought back one hot summer from the Asakusa leather expo in Tokyo, Japan. After making this bag, I closed my eyes, and I could almost smell the soy sauce meatball stand next to Sensō-ji temple.

*Bag* ²

# Retro Camera Bag

Instructions p. 71

I love retro cameras and antiques, so I dyed soft leather an uneven coffee brown and hand stitched all the pieces together to give this bag an antique touch. My studio is called HARUI in Japanese, so I branded an "H" on the front flap to personalize it. Now I use it to hold my retro camera!

 3

# Sunshine Tote

I designed this bag for myself because my favorite color in the whole world is yellow. This bag is like having sunshine at your side all the time! I hand stitched the visible areas and used a sewing machine on the hidden areas to give it a handmade look. At Spring Pig Studios we have leather in every shade and color you can imagine; it's like a beautiful array of brightly colored ice cream in an ice cream shop.

When choosing leather, color and suitability is very important. If you have an attentive and anticipative heart while working, it's bound to show up in your finished design!

Instructions p. 72

   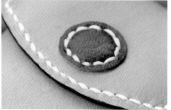

*Bag* **4**

# Sunshine Camera Pouch

My assistant Jo's favorite color is green, so once again we used yellow leather with an added touch of dark green on the button cover to design a camera pouch. The outside is dyed yellow, but we left the natural leather on the inside to protect the camera. On the back of the camera pouch there's a hidden pocket for storing a memory card. I take a lot of pictures, so bringing an extra just-in-case memory card isn't a bad idea.

Instructions p. 74

*Bag* 5

# Envelope Business Card Holder

Instructions p. 75

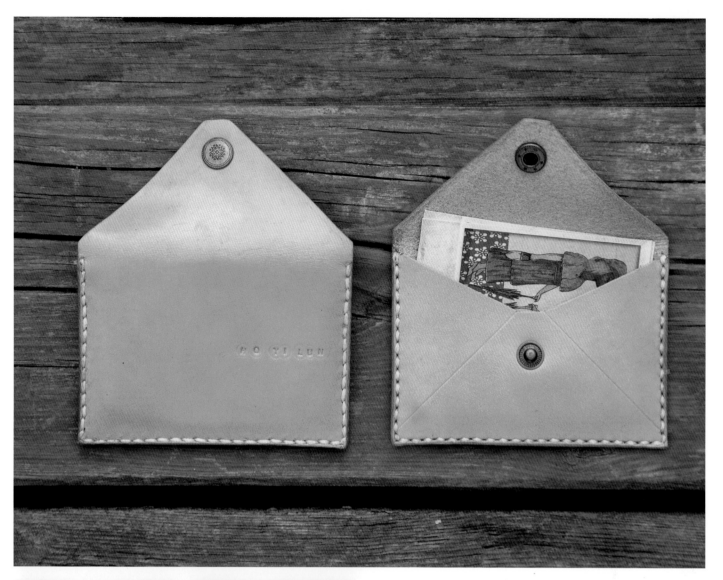

I always forget to bring my business cards with me when I go out, so I usually rely on Mr. Zebra or my assistant to have one on hand at all times. I designed this envelope business card holder so that I'd always want to carry it with me and wouldn't forget to bring my cards along again. You can brand your name on the back to make it even more like an envelope!

*Bag* 6

# British Tartan Bucket Bag

One day, while shopping at Yong-Le market, one of the fabric saleswomen suddenly called me over to her stand. She told me, "This tartan wool fabric is very suitable for you, very British!" I thought for a minute and finally said, "Alright!" Although I've never been to England and know very little about British style, I paired the tartan with leather in hopes that one day I might take it with me on a quest for real British style. It was the saleswoman's warm spirit that sealed the deal!

Instructions p. 76

*Bag 7*

# Embroidered Country Tote

Instructions p. 78

This is the first bag that I designed while studying at Bunka Fashion College. I wasn't so good at embroidery, but I loved to test out lots of different techniques on my work. Being a beginner, this wasn't an easy task. My leather instructor's comments regarding my work were, "She thinks it's even better when the entire bag is covered in embroidery!"

With this bag, the part I'm most satisfied with is the leather pocket on the back. First I embroidered the flowers, then I stitched on the leather pocket. Feel free to change the floral arrangement or even add fruit if you'd like!

*Bag* 8

# Vintage Style Document Folder

Sometimes it isn't usefulness but attractiveness that matters most! I dyed some soft leather an uneven natural tone to give this document folder an antique feel, then branded Spring Pig Studios' Japanese name on the front side. When it was finished, it seemed to me that the folder itself was worth more than the documents it would soon hold. At least this way I won't forget to bring my important documents with me again!

Instructions p. 80

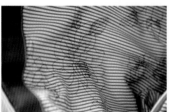

On Mother's Day 2011, I found myself back in Taiwan and made this bag for my mother. I chose her favorite blue leather and branded the words "Happy Mother's Day" and "I love you" on the two inside pockets in hopes that this bag would bring Mom lots of joy on every outing! I designed this bag for her to use for any purpose she desired. She can even use it to take Little Guy (our family's Chihuahua) out and about. For the inside, I chose a soft fabric so that Little Guy would be as snug as a pup in a nest.

*Bag* 9

# All-Purpose Tote

Instructions p. 72

*Bag* 10

# Lunch Bag

I love striped canvas, so when I found this piece I was so excited that I couldn't wait to make an adult-sized lunch bag! I remember when I was young I never carried lunch bags, so I was always jealous of my classmates who carried lunch bags, tin lunch boxes, and steamed rice boxes. To this day I hardly ever carry a lunch bag, but whenever I go out to eat or buy snacks when heading to the movies, this bag really comes in handy!

Instructions p. 81

*Bag* 11

# Lunch Bag (variation)

In another fabric shop I found this striped rainbow canvas and I just couldn't wait to take it home and make a brightly colored lunch bag. I used yellow muntjac leather as a lining for added durability. On both versions of the lunch bag I added a small name card pocket on the front, because accidently taking the wrong lunch box could be a disaster!

Instructions p. 81

Mr. Zebra is big and tall and gets overheated easily, so in order to help him keep cool on hot summer days, I had to choose my materials wisely. When choosing the material, I slid my hand over each piece of fabric because I know that natural fabrics can be prickly and can sometimes ruin cotton clothes if you're not careful. In the end, I chose smooth nylon fabric and added leather accents.

Mr. Zebra and I both have strange tastes in leather. We both like leather that has natural blemishes on it, because it's one of a kind. So for this tote I chose a piece of blemished leather for the front pocket, but if you like perfection you don't have to follow our example.

# Breezy Tote

Instructions p. 83

*Bag* **13**

# Woven Adventure Sling Bag

I love little woven leather bags! They're perfect for carrying your camera, keys, wallet, mosquito repellent, and any other items necessary to set your mind at ease when you're about to embark on an adventure!

Instructions p. 86

There are lots of strips of leather required for this design, so you'll need to be sure your work area is clear of any clutter and prepare some strips of paper and glue before you start. Also, pay special attention to the different lengths of the leather during the weaving process.

*Bag 14*

# Woven Handbag

This is another take on the woven leather bag, only this time with short handles. In Japan, many women like to carry bags similar to this one because shoulder straps and back straps can easily wrinkle clothing. Whether you're going shopping in your favorite dress or just heading to the corner store, this in one handy bag!

Instructions p. 87

The inspiration for this bag came from a student of mine who loved to travel. Although I love good sturdy leather, when traveling for long periods of time I'll always choose a lighter, softer leather instead, because it's easier to manage and doesn't make for a heavy load.

For this bag, I used seven different colors of leather. It's the perfect hobo bag—no matter what you're wearing, it is always a perfect match! The multicolored leather piece I used for this bag isn't my own design—it's a design that I found at the time. You can substitute whatever you can find!

Bag 15

# Suede Hobo Bag

Instructions p. 88

*Bag* 16

# Giant Travel Tote

Ever since I learned to make bags, no matter if its Valentine's Day, a birthday, Christmas, or just celebrating the coming of summer, bags always seem to be the gift I give. This giant travel tote is a bag I made for Mr. Zebra's birthday present. It's simple on the outside, but surprisingly colorful on the inside. Mr. Zebra isn't the one who carries a lot of stuff; on the contrary, it's I who usually has so much with me it's shocking! It's great because when I go shopping, I can just put everything in one giant bag!

Instructions p. 90

This is a piece of leather that has been pressed to look like a woven basket. I don't read books on leather design, but ever since I was a child I have loved to read fables and fairytales. This bag reminds me of Little Red Riding Hood's basket, the kind that you carry flowers and fruit in. Even if you never put it to use, it still makes for a nice home decoration.

*Bag* 17

# Basket Bag

Instructions p. 93

*Bag 18*

# Itsy-Bitsy Book Bag

When I was a student, I always kept my textbooks in a locker at school, so in my book bag I usually would only carry pencils, house keys, a notebook, and my wallet. Back then, if book bags had been this small, students would've loved it! I hand stitched the visible areas on this bag and used a sewing machine on the hidden areas to give it more of a handmade look.

Instructions p. 95

*Bag 19*

# Everyday Tote

What looks like wrinkly blue leather from afar is actually a beautiful, delicate pressed floral design close up. You can use whatever fancy leather you can find. To give this bag unique contrast, I paired the soft blue leather with stiff tan leather handles.

Instructions p. 97

One day I was at a convenience store buying some goods when the checkout clerk asked me if I'd like to buy a one-cent shopping bag. Suddenly, I got to thinking! I rushed back to my studio, scribbled a layout, cut out two pieces of leather, and without even eating lunch, I created this luxury leather shopping bag! I wonder how much it would cost to buy a leather shopping bag? Not one cent!

*Bag 20*

# Luxury Shopping Bag

Instructions p. 98

   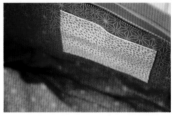

Bag 21

# Healthy Veggies Hobo Bag

I chose this name because during the design process, Mr. Zebra, Jo, and I were thinking about the colors of healthy vegetables. I started with tomato red and added bell pepper green and squash yellow, and together they became the "healthy veggies" hobo bag!

Instructions p. 88

*Bag* 22

# Casual Tote

This is the first piece of black leather that I ever purchased because, aside from leather, I hardly ever wear black clothes. This bag was simply designed to hold whatever is needed for every day.

Instructions p. 99

 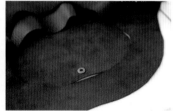 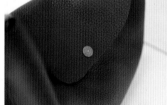

*Bag* **23**

# Dual Strap Messenger Bag

Instructions p. 100

Using the same black leather as the black tote, I designed a dual strap bag. It has two different straps: handles and a shoulder strap. The handles and body are one piece, while the shoulder strap was stitched on separately by hand. You can adjust the length of the straps or the size of the bag to your preference.

*Bag 24*

# Floral Coasters

I love using coasters; they make me feel like I'm at a café. I know it's said that leather shouldn't mix with water, but I think leather coasters still look great over time. Using lots of different kinds of awls to cut out the floral pattern, I started from the center to make the design even. You can change the floral design if you'd like. Don't forget to add the pretty decorative stitches around the edges!

Instructions p. 101

*Bag* 25

# Travel Sling Bag

Instructions p. 102

Every now and then, I'll find a piece of leather with markings left over from the animal's life. To me these aren't blemishes, but precious details that make the piece one of a kind. The shop owner said that this leather once belonged to a cow from South America.

I originally designed this bag for my father to hold his passport and important personal belongings when traveling overseas. When I realized he would only be traveling once or twice a year, I decided to help him keep an eye on it.

*Bag* **26**

# Good Student Backpack

Sometimes I still think backpacks are the way to go. They help evenly distribute the weight you're carrying, and they free up your hands for more useful tasks. The straps on this bag were cut long to make them adjustable. When doing the cutting for this backpack, cut the straps first so there's no worry about not having enough material.

Instructions p. 104

62

*Bag* **27**

# Red Executive Briefcase

Instructions p. 106

Most people carry black briefcases to work; therefore, I chose this red leather with blue suede handle accents as a complement. This way, no matter if you're heading to the office or just simply running errands around town, you can easily stand out in a crowd!

The design is similar to a classic student backpack. Although it may not have back straps, it is still just as durable with a top carry handle allowing you to store many of your personal items. The length and height of the closing flap can be adjusted depending on the position of the buckles you choose.

*Bag 28*

# Monogram Key Sleeves

I branded the letters on these key sleeves and used them to cover my house keys. I remember when I was young I read in stories how evil queens locked princesses up in towers with keys like these. Although I'm not an evil queen, I sure do love my big ring of keys. I've finally made my childhood dreams come true!

Instructions p. 110

# How to Make the Bags

The difference between leather design and embroidery is that no matter if you're punching a hole or sewing a stitch, you never get a second chance! But you mustn't give in simply because of a mistake. Design requires special attention to detail. Follow in Miss Birdy's footsteps and begin your design adventure!

NO 1

# Polka-Dot Clutch

DIFFICULTY: ❤ ❤ ❤

See pattern side C

See pattern side C

**PS.** Remember to pay attention to the width of the leather when cutting!

## Pieces and Supplies

Decorative leather circles x 12

3½" (9cm)

Leather handles x 4
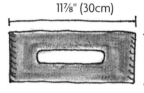
11⅞" (30cm)
4" (10cm)

Lining fabric x 2
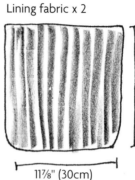
11" (28cm)
11⅞" (30cm)

Outer leather pieces x 2
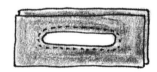
11" (28cm)
11⅞" (30cm)

## Instructions

**1**

Stitch a twirling design on one of the grey circles with a sewing machine.

**2**

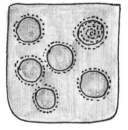

Cut 6 circles out of both blue outer leather pieces and stitch the grey circles on the inner sides.

**3**

After cutting the holes in the handles, stitch each pair of handle pieces together around the hole.

**4**

Place one outer leather piece and one fabric lining piece together with wrong sides facing. Sandwich these between one of the handle pairs, along the bottom edge. Stitch all together, sewing along the bottom edge of the handle. Repeat with the remaining handle pair, outer leather piece, and inner lining piece.

**5** ¼" (0.5cm)

Place each half of the bag with leather outsides facing and stitch the edges together using a ¼" (0.5cm) seam allowance.

**6**

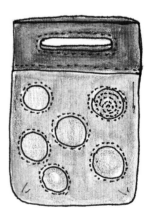

Turn the bag right side out, finish the top edges of the handles, and you're done!

# Retro Camera Bag

DIFFICULTY: ♥♥

See pattern side B

> **Other materials**
> Metal snap (stud and socket)

## Pieces and Supplies

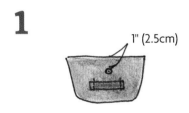

Base strip x 1
10⅞" (27.5cm)
1⅝" (4cm)

Front fastener strips x 2
¾" (2cm)
2¾" (7cm)

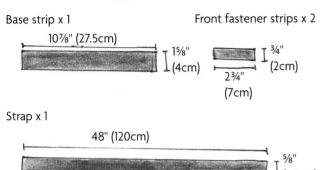

Back and flap piece x 1
5¾" (14.5cm)
7½" (19cm)

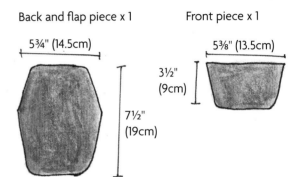

Front piece x 1
5⅜" (13.5cm)
3½" (9cm)

Strap x 1
48" (120cm)
⅝" (1.5cm)

## Instructions

**1**

1" (2.5cm)

Position the snap socket on the right side of the front piece of the case and attach it. Sew on one of the front toggle strips below the snap.

**2**

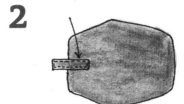

After securing the snap stud to the wrong side of the flap, sew the other toggle strip to the right side of the flap, positioning it as shown.

**3**

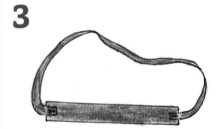

Next, use rivets to attach the base strip to the shoulder strap.

**4**

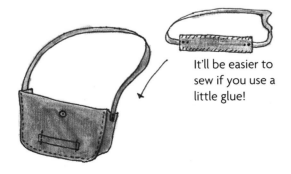

It'll be easier to sew if you use a little glue!

Use leather adhesive to attach the front piece to the base strip with wrong sides facing, then sew them together.

**5**

Finally, attach the back and flap leather piece to the base strip with wrong sides facing, using the same method. Sew them together, and you're done!

# Sunshine Tote

See pattern side C

# All-Purpose Tote

DIFFICULTY: ♥ ♥ ♥

See pattern side D

**PS**. Illustrated are the pieces and instructions for the Sunshine Tote. The All-Purpose Tote patterns appear on pattern side D, and are not illustrated here.

## Pieces and Supplies

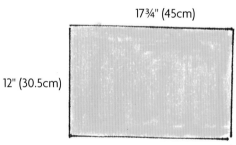

17¾" (45cm)

12" (30.5cm)

Main outer leather pieces x 2

Inside rim pieces x 2

17¾" (45cm)

1¾" (4.5cm)

Straps strips x 4

26" (66cm)

1¼" (3cm)

Outer leather strips for bottom x 2

17¾" (45cm)

2¾" (7cm)

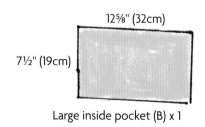

12⅝" (32cm)

7½" (19cm)

Large inside pocket (B) x 1

Base leather x 1

13⅜" (34cm)

4" (10cm)

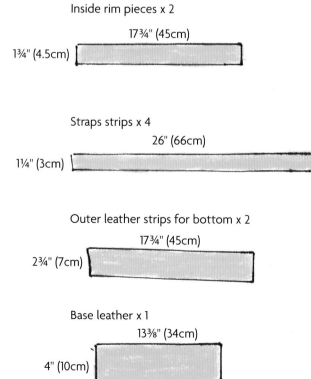

Inside pen pocket strip x 1

4" (10cm)

2" (5cm)

Small inside pocket (A) x 1

5⅛" (13cm)

4" (10cm)

Card pocket plastic window x 1

3½" (9cm)

2⅜" (6cm)

Card pocket x 1

4⅜" (11cm)

2¾" (7cm)

Main lining fabric x 2

17¾" (45cm)

11½" (29cm)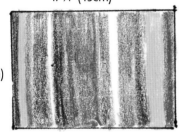

Lining fabric for large inside pocket (B) x 1

12⅝" (32cm)

7⅛" (18cm)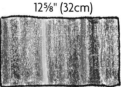

Base lining fabric x 1

13⅜" (34cm)

4" (10cm)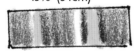

Lining fabric for small inside pocket (A) x 1

5⅛" (13cm)

3½" (9cm)

# Instructions

## 1

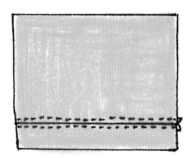

Sew one main outer piece and one base leather piece together with right sides facing using a ⅜" (1cm) seam allowance. Glue the seam allowance open with leather adhesive. On the right side, top stitch on each side of the seam to create decorative stitching. Repeat with the remaining outer and base pieces.

## 2

The Sunshine Tote and the All-Purpose Tote are constructed similarly. Look at the photos and pattern pieces to understand the construction of the All-Purpose Tote. Refer to the Red Executive Briefcase, page 106, for additional instructions.

# Sunshine Camera Pouch

DIFFICULTY: ❤ ❤ ❤

See pattern side B

## Pieces and Supplies

Main leather body x 1
Raw leather lining x 1

13⅜" (34cm)

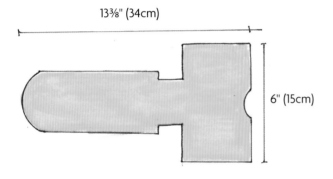

6" (15cm)

Memory card pocket fastener flap x 1

¾" (2cm)

1¾"
(4.5cm)

Memory card pocket x 1

1⅝" (4cm)

1¾"
(4.5cm)

Memory card pocket fastener strip x 1

1⅝" (4cm)

⅜" (1cm)

Magnet cover circles x 2

1" (2.5cm)

## Instructions

**1**

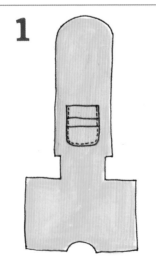

First, hand stich the memory card pocket and fastener strip onto the main body of the case.

**2**

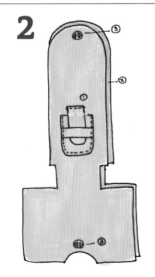

1. Sew on the fastener flap.
2. Glue the raw leather lining to the main leather body with wrong sides facing. **3.** When the glue is dry, attach the magnet snap pieces.

**3**

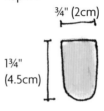

3⅜"
(8.5cm)

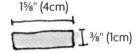

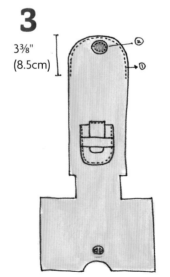

1. Hand stich the cover and lining together on the flap only.
2. Sew the green snap covers on over the backs of the snaps.

**4**

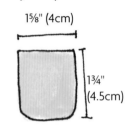

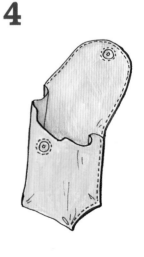

Finally, stich the edges of the body together, apply a layer of black edging oil, and you're done!

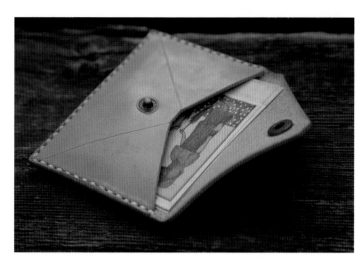

# Envelope Business Card Holder

**DIFFICULTY:** ♥

See pattern side C

## Pieces and Supplies

Main body piece x 1

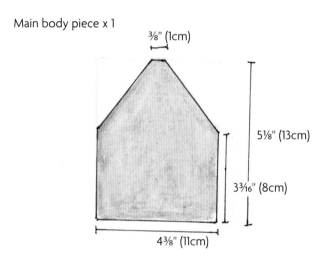

⅜" (1cm)

5⅛" (13cm)

3³⁄₁₆" (8cm)

4⅜" (11cm)

Front piece x 1

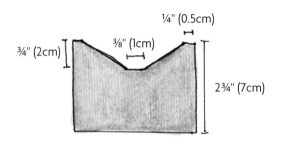

¼" (0.5cm)

⅜" (1cm)

¾" (2cm)

2¾" (7cm)

## Instructions

### 1

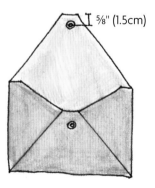

⅝" (1.5cm)

Draw two lines on the right side of the front piece to give it the folded envelope look. After that, attach the snap socket and stud to their appropriate pieces and punch holes along the edges of both pieces with an awl in order to sew them together.

### 2

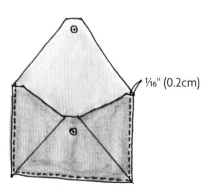

¹⁄₁₆" (0.2cm)

After you've made the holes, you can sew the pieces together. If you plan to carry many cards, you can widen the envelope. You can even brand your name on the front to get a real envelope effect.

# British Tartan Bucket Bag

DIFFICULTY: ♥♥

See pattern side C

### Other materials
Metal snaps (stud and socket) x 2
Rivets x 4

## Pieces and Supplies

Side fabric x 2

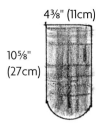

4⅜" (11cm)

10⅝" (27cm)

Front and back fabric x 2

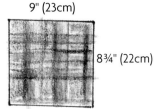

9" (23cm)

8¾" (22cm)

Lining fabric x 2

9" (23cm)

11½" (29cm)

Base leather x 1

9" (23cm)

3½" (9cm)

Handle strips x 4

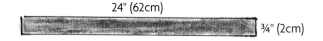

24" (62cm)

¾" (2cm)

Front and back leather x 2

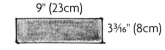

9" (23cm)

3³⁄₁₆" (8cm)

Lining fabric for base x 1

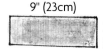

9" (23cm)

3³⁄₁₆" (8cm)

## Instructions

### 1

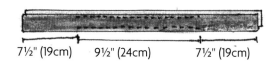

7½" (19cm)    9½" (24cm)    7½" (19cm)

First glue each pair of handle strips together with wrong sides facing. Then sew them together along the marked section using a ⅛" (0.3cm) seam allowance. Leave 7½" (19cm) unstitched on each end.

### 2

3" (7.5cm)

Position the straps on the front and back fabric pieces. You can use double-sided tape to keep them in place while stitching.

### 3

Then sew the straps onto the fabric using a sewing machine. Pick up where you left off with the stitching in step 1.

## 4

Fold the front and back leather pieces down ¼" (0.5cm) and glue the edge down.

## 5

Then, take each of the ¼" (0.5cm) folded edges, glue them ⅜" (1cm) up from the bottom of the front and back fabric pieces, and sew them on using a ¼" (0.5cm) allowance.

## 6

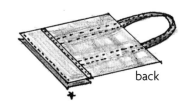

back

Sew the base to the bottom of front bag piece with right sides facing, using a ¼" (0.5cm) allowance.

## 7

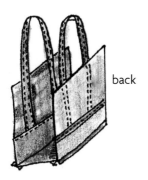

back

Sew the other side of the base to the bottom of the back bag piece with right sides facing, and turn the bag inside out.

## 8

⅜" (1cm)

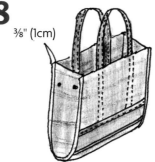

Attach the snaps to both sides of each of the side fabric pieces and sew the sides onto the front and back pieces using a ⅜" (1cm) seam allowance. Be sure that the bag is still inside out during this stage and that you sew the pieces together with right sides facing.

## 9

Turn the bag right side out and fold the edges of the mouth of the bag down about ⅜" (1cm).

## 10

Sew the lining together using the same method as the bag, using a ⅜"–½" (1–1.2cm) seam allowance. Turn the lining inside out and fold the edges of the mouth down ⅜" (1cm) toward the wrong side.

## 11

⅜" (1cm)

Place the lining into the body of the bag with wrong sides facing and sew the two together using a ¼" (0.5cm) allowance. Finally, add rivets ⅜" (1cm) down from the mouth of the bag to reinforce the handles. You're done!

# Embroidered Country Tote

DIFFICULTY: ♥ ♥

See pattern side C

## Other materials
4 rivets
1 metal snap (stud and socket)
Embroidery thread, stamps, ink

## Pieces and Supplies

Main fabric front and back x 2

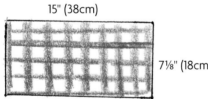

15" (38cm)

7⅞" (20cm)

Leather base x 1
Base lining fabric x 1

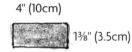

10½" (26.5cm)

4½" (11.5cm)

Lining fabric x 2

15" (38cm)

7⅛" (18cm)

Leather flowerpot pocket top x 1

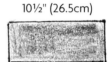

4" (10cm)

1⅜" (3.5cm)

Leather flowerpot pocket bottom x 1

3½" (9cm)

3½" (9cm)

Inside pocket fabric x 1

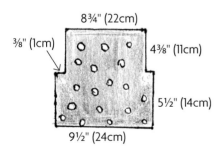

8¾" (22cm)

⅜" (1cm)

4⅜" (11cm)

5½" (14cm)

9½" (24cm)

Handle strips x 4

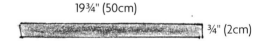

19¾" (50cm)

¾" (2cm)

Inside rim leather pieces x 2

15" (38cm)

1¼" (3cm)

# Instructions

## 1

Fold top edge over
¼" (0.5cm)

1¼" (3cm)

2⅜" (6cm)

Sew on using a ⅜" (1cm) seam allowance.

First embroider your pattern onto both sides of the main fabric. Assemble the leather flowerpot separately, place it over the base of your embroidered flowers to give them a potted plant look, and sew it on.

## 2

The design of the body of this bag is similar to other bags in this book. Refer to the Red Executive Briefcase, page 106, for instructions.

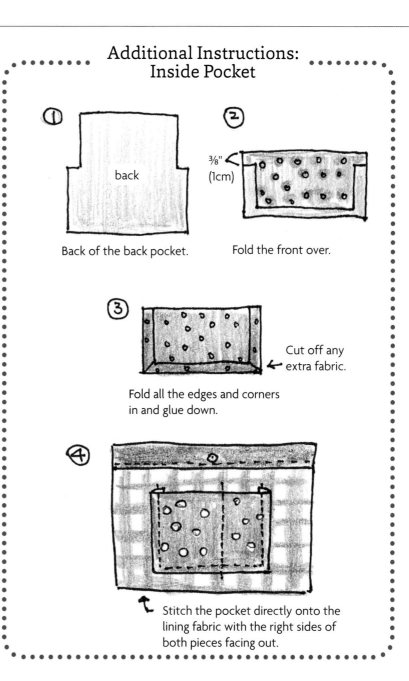

### Additional Instructions: Inside Pocket

① back

Back of the back pocket.

② ⅜" (1cm)

Fold the front over.

③ Cut off any extra fabric.

Fold all the edges and corners in and glue down.

④ Stitch the pocket directly onto the lining fabric with the right sides of both pieces facing out.

# Vintage Style Document Folder

DIFFICULTY: ♥

See pattern side B

**Other materials**
Metal snaps (stud and socket) x 2

## Pieces and Supplies

Back pieces x 2

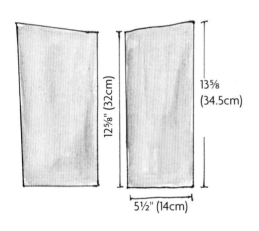

12⅝" (32cm)

13⅝ (34.5cm)

5½" (14cm)

Front piece x 1

15⅜" (39cm)

10½" (26.5cm)

Card pocket x 1

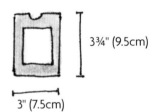

3¾" (9.5cm)

3" (7.5cm)

Card pocket plastic window x 1

2⅝" (6.5cm)

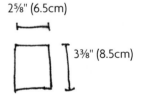

3⅜" (8.5cm)

## Instructions

**1**

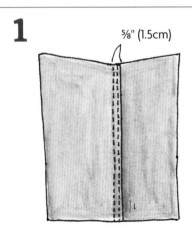

⅝" (1.5cm)

Overlap the two back pieces about ⅝" (1.5cm) and use two lines of stitches to sew them together.

**2**

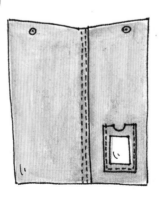

Glue the plastic window to the wrong side of the card pocket, hand stitch the pocket to the back piece, and attach the snap sockets.

**3**

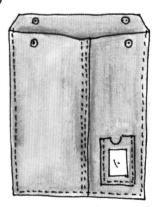

Sew the front and back together with wrong sides facing, attach the snap studs, and you're done!

# Lunch Bag

# Lunch Bag (variation)

DIFFICULTY: ♥♥

See pattern side D

## Other materials
Metal snaps (stud and socket) x 2
Plastic window
Fabric cable

## Pieces and Supplies

17⅜" (44cm)

8¾"
(22cm)

Main fabric pieces x 2

18⅛" (46cm)

1⅝"
(4cm)

Handle strips x 2

3³⁄₁₆" (8cm)   17⅜" (44cm)

4⅛" (10.5cm)    7½" (19cm)

Leather base x 1

Leather name
window piece x 1

17⅜" (44cm)

2" (5cm)

Inside rim leather pieces x 2

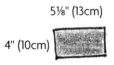

6¼" (16cm)

4" (10cm)

Outside leather pocket x 1

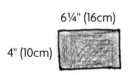

5⅛" (13cm)

4" (10cm)

Large inside leather pocket x 1

2¾" (7cm)

4" (10cm)

Small inside leather
pocket x 1

17⅜" (44cm)

9½"
(24cm)

Lining fabric x 2

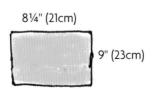

8¼" (21cm)

9" (23cm)

Base lining fabric x 1

# Instructions

## 1

Glue the plastic window to the wrong side of the leather window piece, and sew it onto the right side of one of the main fabric pieces. Sew the outside leather pocket onto the other.

## 2

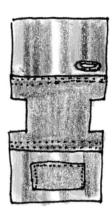

Overlap the fabric with the leather by about ½" (1.2cm) and sew two rows of stitches, one ¼" (0.5cm) from the edge of the leather, and one ⅜" (1cm) from the edge of the leather to attach them.

## 3

1⅝" (4cm)

1/16" (0.2cm)

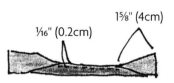

For the handles, fold each piece in half lengthwise and sew a 15" (38cm) section of the open edge as shown, using a 1/16" (0.2cm) seam allowance. Leave 1⅝" (4cm) unsewn on both ends. Then pull the fabric cord through the handle (or, if you don't like this effect, you can omit the cord).

## 4

Glue the handles inside the mouth of the bag and attach each set of metal snaps to each side of the bag (similarly to the British Tartan Bucket Bag, page 76). The design of the body of this bag is similar to other bags in this book. Remember to fold the mouth of the bag down ⅜" (1cm) before gluing on the handles.

## 5

Sew the inside pockets onto the lining however you like. You can refer to the Giant Travel Tote, page 90, as an example.

## 6

Place the lining in the bag with wrong sides facing, sew on the lining and inside rim pieces using a ¼" (0.5cm) allowance, and you're done!

# Breezy Tote

DIFFICULTY: ❤❤❤

See pattern side C

## Pieces and Supplies

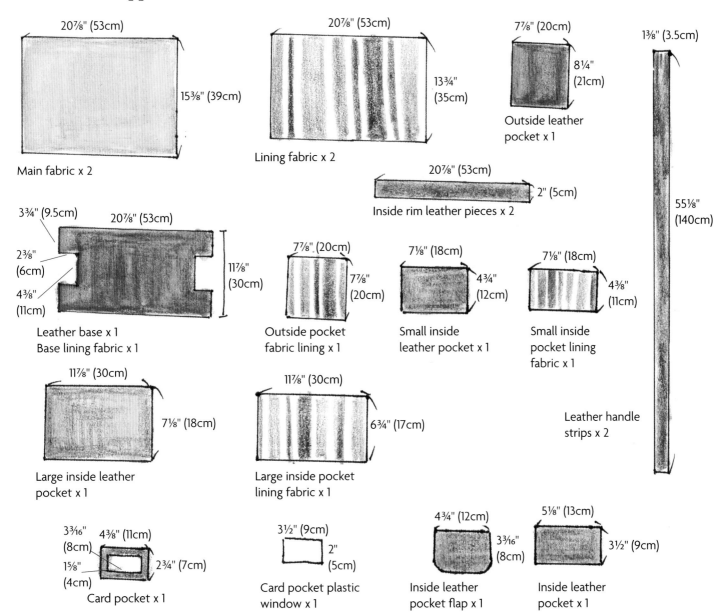

20⅞" (53cm)

15⅜" (39cm)

Main fabric x 2

20⅞" (53cm)

13¾" (35cm)

Lining fabric x 2

7⅞" (20cm)

8¼" (21cm)

Outside leather pocket x 1

1⅜" (3.5cm)

55⅛" (140cm)

3¾" (9.5cm)

2⅜" (6cm)

20⅞" (53cm)

4⅜" (11cm)

11⅞" (30cm)

Leather base x 1
Base lining fabric x 1

20⅞" (53cm)

2" (5cm)

Inside rim leather pieces x 2

7⅞" (20cm)

7⅞" (20cm)

Outside pocket fabric lining x 1

7⅛" (18cm)

4¾" (12cm)

Small inside leather pocket x 1

7⅛" (18cm)

4⅜" (11cm)

Small inside pocket lining fabric x 1

Leather handle strips x 2

11⅞" (30cm)

7⅛" (18cm)

Large inside leather pocket x 1

11⅞" (30cm)

6¾" (17cm)

Large inside pocket lining fabric x 1

3³⁄₁₆" (8cm)

4⅜" (11cm)

1⅝" (4cm)

2¾" (7cm)

Card pocket x 1

3½" (9cm)

2" (5cm)

Card pocket plastic window x 1

4¾" (12cm)

3³⁄₁₆" (8cm)

Inside leather pocket flap x 1

5⅛" (13cm)

3½" (9cm)

Inside leather pocket x 1

# Instructions

**1**

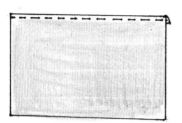

Fold the tops of the two main fabric pieces down ⅜" (1cm) and sew the fold in place.

**2**

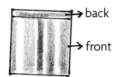

back

front

Place the outside pocket lining and outside leather pocket together with wrong sides facing.

**3**

back

Fold the top of the leather piece over toward the lining side ¼" (0.5cm) and stitch in place.

**4**

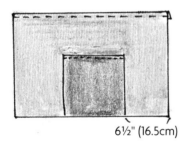

6½" (16.5cm)

Place the pocket onto the front of one of the main fabric pieces.

**5**

Place one shoulder strap, overlapping the pocket sides about ⅜" (1cm), and sew them to the front of the fabric using a ⅛" (0.3cm) allowance. Sew the remaining shoulder strap to the back fabric piece.

**6**

Fold the long edges of the leather base over ⅜" (1cm) and glue down.

**7**

Sew the folded edges of the base to the main fabric pieces using a ¼" (0.5cm) allowance. Because the bag is very large, you can ruche slightly when sewing on the base.

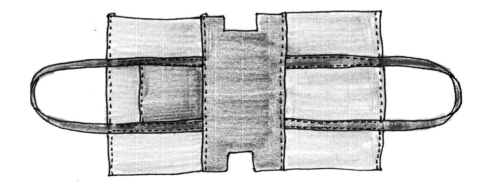

**8**

After sewing the body of the bag together, turn the bag right side out (refer to Red Executive Briefcase, page 106).

**9**

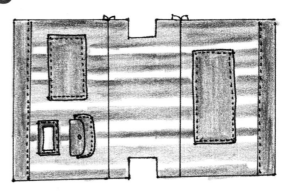

Sew on the lined inside pockets using the same method as you did with the outside pocket.

**10**

The seam allowances are ¾" (2cm) in width; if they're too thick, trim them a bit.

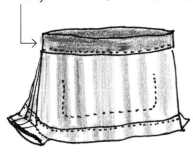

Refer to Red Executive Briefcase, page 106, for the instructions on how to sew the lining.

**11**

⅝" (1.5cm)

Place the finished lining into the body of the bag with wrong sides facing and sew them together using a ⅜" (1cm) allowance. Finally, place four rivets on the handles for reinforcement about ⅝" (1.5cm) down from the mouth of the bag. You're done!

# Woven Adventure Sling Bag

DIFFICULTY: ❤❤❤

See pattern side C

## Pieces and Supplies

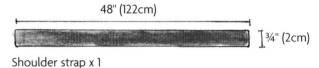

48" (122cm)

¾" (2cm)

Shoulder strap x 1

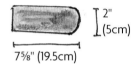

2" (5cm)

7⅝" (19.5cm)

Fastener flap x 2

## Instructions

**1**

For weaving instructions, please refer to Woven Handbag, page 87.

**2**

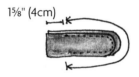

1⅝" (4cm)

Using a ¼" (0.5cm) seam allowance, hand stitch the two pieces of the leather fastener flap together with wrong sides facing, leaving 1⅝" (4cm) unstitched on the flat end.

**3**

After attaching the buckle to the rounded edge, coat the edges of the leather fastener with edging oil.

**4**

After trimming the mouth of the bag, attach the fastener flap.

**5**

The top two seam allowances are ¾" (2cm); if they are too thick, they can be trimmed.

For instructions on the construction of the lining, refer to Red Executive Briefcase, page 106.

**6**

Finally, attach the shoulder strap using rivets and insert the lining into the body of the bag. Sew it all together, and you're done!

# Woven Handbag

DIFFICULTY: ♥ ♥ ♥

## Pieces and Supplies

Both woven bags have the same body shape, but the shoulder straps and handles are different.

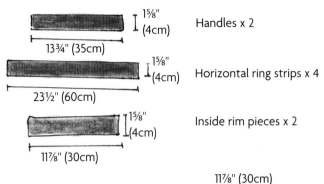

13¾" (35cm) · 1⅝" (4cm) — Handles x 2

23½" (60cm) · 1⅝" (4cm) — Horizontal ring strips x 4

11⅞" (30cm) · 1⅝" (4cm) — Inside rim pieces x 2

### Vertical strips x 5

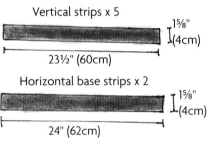

23½" (60cm) · 1⅝" (4cm)

### Horizontal base strips x 2

24" (62cm) · 1⅝" (4cm)

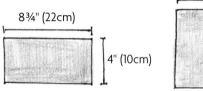

8¾" (22cm) · 4" (10cm)

Base lining fabric x 1

11⅞" (30cm) · 4⅜" (11cm)

Lining fabric x 2

## Instructions

**1**

Weave five vertical strips and two horizontal base strips together, centering them all.

**2**

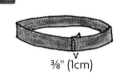

⅜" (1cm)

Make a loop with each of the horizontal ring strips and sew the ends of each strip together.

**3**

Take the horizontal ring strips and weave them into the vertical strips, remembering to hide the seams. Then fold down the leftover leather at the top.

**4**

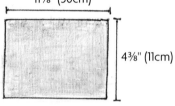

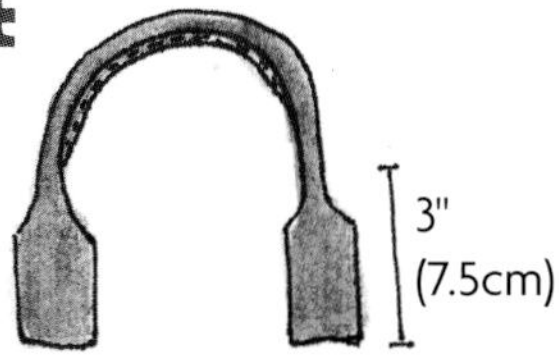

3" (7.5cm)

Fold the handles in half lengthwise and sew along the center of the open edge using a ⅛"–¼" (0.3–0.5cm) seam allowance, leaving 3" (7.5cm) unstitched on each end.

**5**

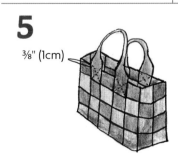

⅜" (1cm)

Hand stitch the handles onto the front of the bag using a box stitch.

**6**

The top two seam allowances are ¾" (2cm). If they are too thick, they can be trimmed.

For instructions on the construction of the lining, please refer to Red Executive Briefcase, page 106. Add metal snaps to the center of the inner rim pieces.

**7**

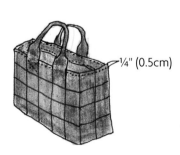

¼" (0.5cm)

Finally, place the lining into the body of the bag. Sew them together, and you're done!

# Suede Hobo Bag

**PS.** These two bags are exactly the same shape, but the Healthy Veggies Hobo Bag has an extra pocket. The inside and outside are the same, but the stitching differs by 3⁄8"–1⁄2" (1–1.2cm).

# Healthy Veggies Hobo Bag

DIFFICULTY: ♥ ♥ ♥

See pattern side A

**Other materials**
Metal loops for straps x 2
19¾" (50cm) zipper x 1

Base x 1

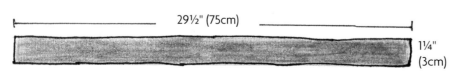

35½" (90cm)

Front and back pieces x 2

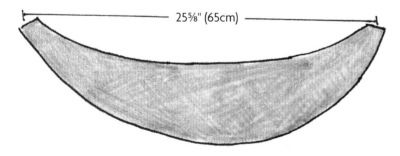

25⅝" (65cm)

Shoulder strap x 1

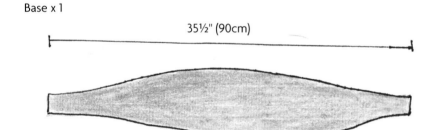

29½" (75cm)

1¼"
(3cm)

Shoulder strap decorative strip x 1

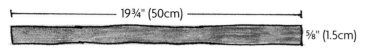

19¾" (50cm)

⅝" (1.5cm)

Strap tabs x 2

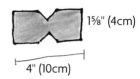

1⅝" (4cm)

4" (10cm)

Zipper cover x 1

3⁄8" (1cm)

19⅞" (50.5cm)

1⅝" (4cm)

25⅜" (65cm)

## Instructions

**1**

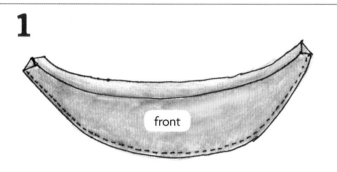

front

Sew the front, back, and base together.

**2**

Sew the zipper to the leather cover, leaving ¼" (0.5cm) on either end.

**3**

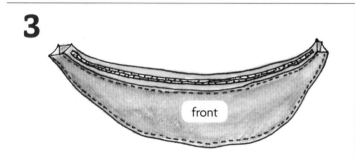

front

Open the zipper and sew the piece to the bag mouth.

**4**

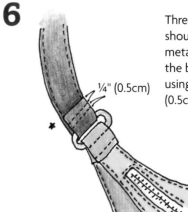

front

Next, sew the strap tabs onto each corner of the bag, sandwiching the base and the zipper cover between the tab ends. Don't forget to add the metal strap loops.

**5**

Sew the decorative stitching along the shoulder strap, then sew the decorative leather strip onto the shoulder strap, using a 1⁄16"-1⁄8" (0.2-0.3cm) seam allowance all around.

**6**

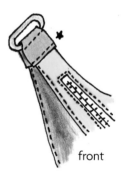

¼" (0.5cm)

Thread the ends of the shoulder strap through the metal loops on either side of the bag and sew them in place using two lines of stitches ¼" (0.5cm) apart, as shown.

# Giant Travel Tote

DIFFICULTY: ♥ ♥ ♥

See pattern side B

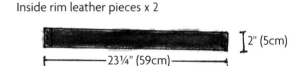 → This means thin the edges with a razor.

## Pieces and Supplies

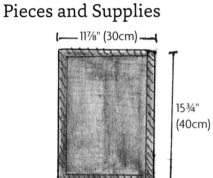

11⅞" (30cm)

15¾" (40cm)

Main leather front and back pieces x 4

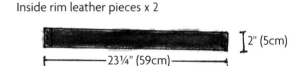 Thin the edges

23¼" (59cm)

4¾" (12cm)

1⅝" (4cm)

2¾" (7cm)

Leather base x 1

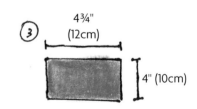 1¼" (3cm)

Leather snap base x 1

6¼" (16cm)

¾" (2cm)

Key loop x 1

Shoulder straps strips x 4

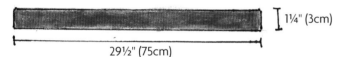 1¼" (3cm)

29½" (75cm)

Inside rim leather pieces x 2

 2" (5cm)

23¼" (59cm)

Inner leather pockets (3) x 1 each

① 4¾" (12cm)

2¾" (7cm)

② 10⅝" (27cm)

7⅞" (20cm)

③ 4¾" (12cm)

4" (10cm)

23¼" (59cm)

14⅝" (37cm)

Main lining fabric x 2

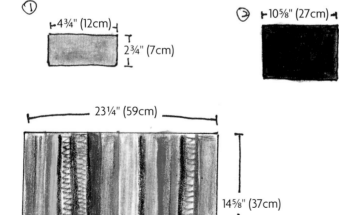

17¾" (45cm)

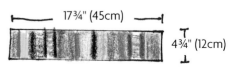 4¾" (12cm)

Base lining fabric x 1

# Instructions

### 1

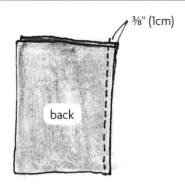

⅜" (1cm)

back

Place double-sided tape on the right sides of the main leather pieces.

### 2

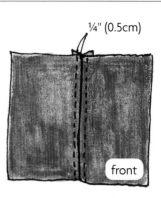

¼" (0.5cm)

front

With right sides facing, sew a seam down one long edge of the main leather pieces, then remove the tape. Open the pieces and glue the seam allowances down using leather adhesive, and sew two decorative lines down either side of the seam on the right side.

### 3

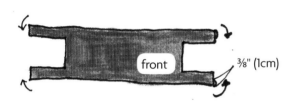

front

⅜" (1cm)

Fold down the top and bottom edges of the base ⅜" (1cm) and glue down with leather adhesive.

### 4

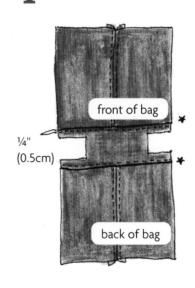

front of bag

¼" (0.5cm)

back of bag

After folding the base, sew the folded edges to the front sides of the main leather pieces. The bag is huge, so you need to be careful not to knock things over when sewing.

### 5

Remember to open the edges on → either side. The top ¾" (2cm) can be trimmed.

With right sides facing, sew the body together using a ¼" (0.5cm) seam allowance.

### 6

Turn the bag right side out and fold the mouth of the bag down ⅜" (1cm).

## 7

⅛"–³⁄₁₆"
(0.3–0.4cm)

Glue each pair of leather strap strips together (wrong sides facing) with leather adhesive for each shoulder strap, then sew them together along the long edges.

## 8

2" (5cm)

Next, glue the shoulder straps inside the mouth of the bag about 2" (5cm) down. After punching holes for the thread with an awl, hand-stitch the straps to the bag using a box stitch.

## 9

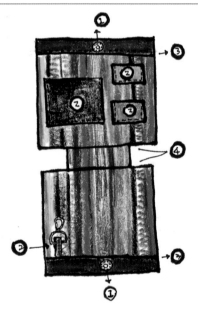

## Lining

**1.** First, attach the metal socket snap on the leather snap base, and sew the leather snap base and its corresponding stud to the rim pieces.

**2.** Then, sew the three pockets to the inside lining and sew decorative stitches on the key loop.

**3.** Next, sew the inside rim leather pieces and the lining pieces together, placing the key loop between the leather and fabric to stitch it in place.

**4.** Sew the lining sides and the lining base together to complete.

## 10

The top two seam allowances are ¾" (2cm); if they are too thick, they can be trimmed.

back

Sew the lining together the same way you sewed the body together, using a ⅜"–½" (1–1.2cm) allowance.

## 11

¼" (0.5cm)

Place the lining in the body of the bag, stitch them together using a ¼" (0.5cm) allowance, and you're done!

# Basket Bag

**DIFFICULTY:** ♥ ♥

See pattern side A

**Other materials**
Rivets x 8

## Pieces and Supplies

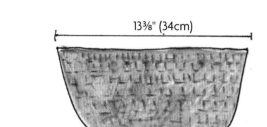

13⅜" (34cm)

Main leather pieces x 2

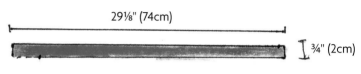

29⅛" (74cm)

¾" (2cm)

Edging strip x 1

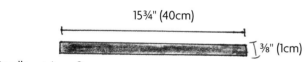

15¾" (40cm)

⅜" (1cm)

Handles strips x 2

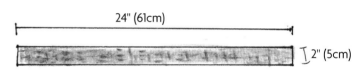

24" (61cm)

2" (5cm)

Base leather x 1

## Instructions

### 1

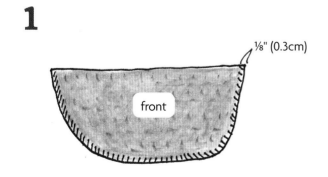

⅛" (0.3cm)

front

Stick double-sided tape to the right side of one of the main pieces of leather.

### 2

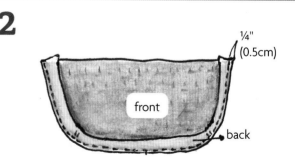

¼" (0.5cm)

front

back

With right sides facing, position the base along the edge and sew them together.

**3**

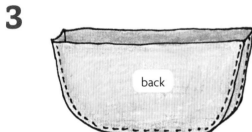

back

Sew on the second main piece of leather to the base with right sides facing. After all three pieces are sewn together, the body of the bag is assembled inside out.

**4**

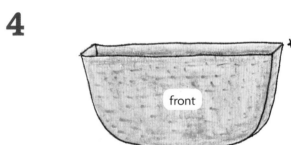

front

Gently turn the bag right side out.

**5**

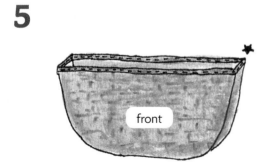

front

Next, fold the thin edging strip over the top edge of the bag and stitch it in place.

**6**

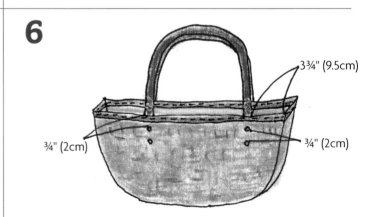

3¾" (9.5cm)

¾" (2cm)

¾" (2cm)

Finally, attach the handles to the inside of the bag mouth using the rivets. You're done!

# Itsy-Bitsy Book Bag

DIFFICULTY: ♥ ♥

See pattern side A

## Pieces and Supplies

Outer leather flap x 1

10⅝" (27cm)

6¼" (16cm)

Flap leather lining x 1

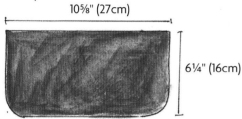

2⅝" (6.5cm)

10⅝" (27cm)

Leather flap strips x 2

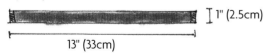

1" (2.5cm)

13" (33cm)

Handle strips x 2

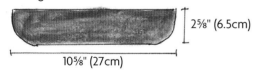

1" (2.5cm)

7⅛" (18cm)

  Thin the edges

12¼" (31cm)

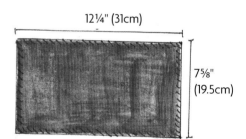

7⅝" (19.5cm)

Main leather pieces x 2

7⅞" (20cm)

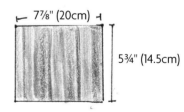

5¾" (14.5cm)

Lining fabric x 2

20½" (52cm)

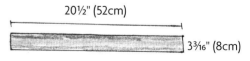

3³⁄₁₆" (8cm)

Base lining fabric x 1

8¾" (22cm)

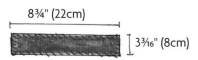

3³⁄₁₆" (8cm)

Leather base x 1

7⅞" (20cm)

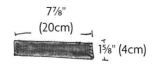

1⅝" (4cm)

Inside rim leather pieces x 2

3³⁄₁₆" (8cm)

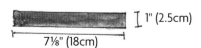

1⅝" (4cm)

Additional inside rim leather pieces x 2
(for left and right sides)

# Instructions

## 1

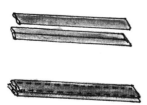

First, fold down the long edges of the handle strips, glue down, and sew together along the long edges using a ¼" (0.5cm) seam allowance.

## 2

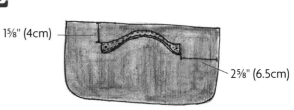

1⅝" (4cm)

2⅝" (6.5cm)

Position the handle on the outer leather flap piece and attach using rivets.

## 3

Fold down ¼" (0.5cm).

1⅜" (3.5cm)

4⅜" (11cm)

Fold the ends back up to about ¼" (0.5cm) under the flap.

Position the flap strips on the flap on either side of the handle. Fold the ends under and sew them in place using a ⅛" (0.3cm) allowance. Punch holes in the strips to receive the metal studs.

## 4

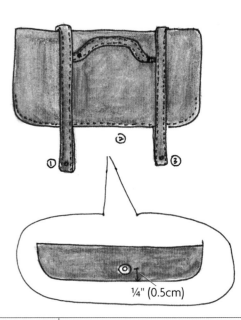

① ② ③

¼" (0.5cm)

Position the metal stud and socket snap (2) on the back side of the flap, ¼" (0.5cm) away from the edge of the flap, and attach. Attach the snap covers (1) and (2) for the studs on the main bag body on the holes created in the flap strips.

## 5

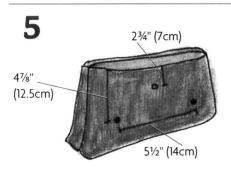

2¾" (7cm)

4⅞" (12.5cm)

5½" (14cm)

For instructions on the construction of the body, refer to Red Executive Briefcase, page 106. Remember to attach the two studs and one socket to the front of the bag and to fold the mouth of the bag down ⅜" (1cm).

## 6

After the body of the bag and the flap are assembled, sew the flap onto the body of the bag, positioning the flap ⅜" (1cm) down from the top of the back side. Sew together with two lines of stitches with ¼" (0.5cm) between them for durability.

## 7

Place the lining inside the body of the bag and sew together using a ¼" (0.5cm) allowance. You're done!

# Everyday Tote

DIFFICULTY: ♥♥

See pattern side A

## Pieces and Supplies

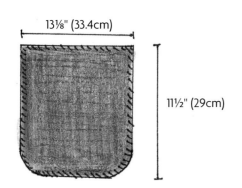

13⅛" (33.4cm)

11½" (29cm)

Main leather pieces x 2

20⅞" (53cm)

⅝" (1.5cm)

Handles x 2

33⅞" (86cm)

2" (5cm)

Base x 1

## Instructions

### 1

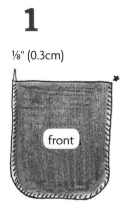

⅛" (0.3cm)

front

Apply a ⅛" (0.3cm) wide line of double-sided tape around the edges of the front piece of leather.

### 2

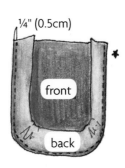

¼" (0.5cm)

front

back

Then, attach the base to the front with right sides facing and sew together using a ¼" (0.5cm) seam allowance.

### 3

back

Using the same method, attach the second piece of leather to the base, right sides facing.

### 4

⅜" (1cm)

front

Next, turn the bag right side out and fold the mouth of the bag down ⅜" (1cm). Glue the rim down and sew using a ¼" (0.5cm) allowance.

### 5

3³⁄₁₆" (8cm)

⅜" (1cm)

Finally, glue the handles to the inside of the bag, punch holes for the thread with an awl, and sew them on.

# Luxury Shopping Bag

DIFFICULTY: ♥

See pattern side B

## Pieces and Supplies

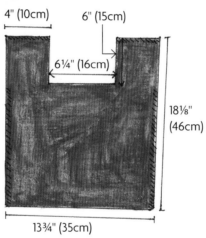

4" (10cm)

6" (15cm)

6¼" (16cm)

18⅛" (46cm)

13¾" (35cm)

Main leather pieces x 2

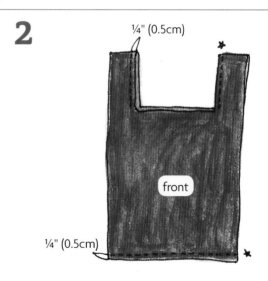

Thin the edges

## Instructions

### 1

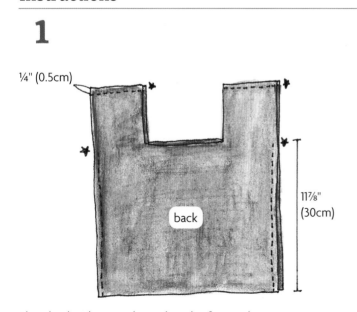

¼" (0.5cm)

back

11⅞" (30cm)

Place both sides together right sides facing, then sew across the tops of the handles and up both sides to 11⅞" (30cm) from the bottom.

### 2

¼" (0.5cm)

front

¼" (0.5cm)

Turn the bag right side out, and then hand stitch across the base and along the edges of the handles. You're finished!

 NO 22

# Casual Tote

DIFFICULTY: ♥

See pattern side A

## Other materials
Metal snap (stud and socket) x 1

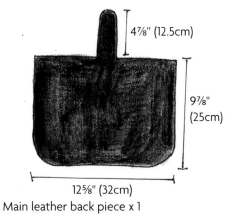

4⅞" (12.5cm)

9⅞" (25cm)

12⅝" (32cm)
Main leather back piece x 1

## Pieces and Supplies

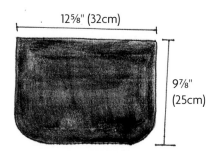

12⅝" (32cm)

9⅞" (25cm)

Main leather front piece x 1

20½" (52cm)

1⅜" (3.5cm)

Handles x 2

## Instructions

### 1

front

First cut the top of both outer pieces of leather with pinking shears for a decorative edge. Then, with right sides facing, glue the edges together about ⅛" (0.3cm) on each side.

### 2

back

After gluing, sew the pieces together along the edges using a ¼" (0.5cm) seam allowance.

### 3

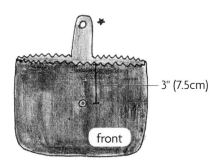

3" (7.5cm)

front

After stitching, turn the bag right side out, and attach the metal snap stud and socket to the fastener and bag front.

### 4

Finally, sew the hand straps inside the bag mouth, and you're done!

# Dual Strap Messenger Bag

DIFFICULTY: ♥

See pattern side A

## Pieces and Supplies

Main leather front piece x 1

Main leather back piece x 1

26¾" (68cm)

1⅝" (4cm)

Shoulder strap x 1

## Instructions

**1**

front

Using the handle hole in the main front piece of leather as a guide, cut an arc in the main back piece of leather to create a flap.

**2**

back

With right sides facing, glue the main pieces together ⅛" (0.3cm) around the rim, then sew together using a ¼" (0.5cm) seam allowance.

**3**

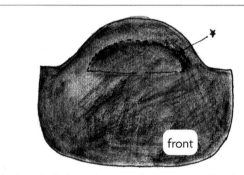

Turn the bag right side out, and attach a metal snap stud and socket to the flap and bag front.

**4**

Finally, hand stitch the shoulder strap to either side of the bag body. The built-in handles can be tucked inside the bag when not in use.

# Floral Coasters

DIFFICULTY: ♥

## Pieces and Supplies
• 4" (10cm) diameter circles of stiff leather
• Awls and hole punches
• Large needle, thread, and diamond
  hole punch

## Instructions

### 1

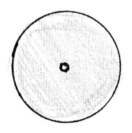

Before punching holes in your coasters, first find the center of the circle. If you brand out from the center, your design will be more organized. You'll need to use the tools you have and your creativity to make each design different!

### 2

You can hand stich a line around the edges to add an even stronger handmade effect.

# Travel Sling Bag

DIFFICULTY: ♥♥

See pattern side D

## Other materials
Front buckle x 1
Metal loops x 2
Shoulder strap buckle x 1
Rivets x 2

## Pieces and Supplies

Main leather pieces x 2 — 9" (23cm) × 11¼" (28.5cm)

Outer flap x 1 — 8½" (21.5cm) × 7⅞" (20cm)

Flap leather lining x 1 — 8½" (21.5cm) × 3¾" (9.5cm)

Lining fabric x 2 — 9" (23cm) × 9½" (24cm)

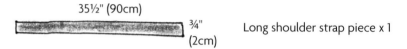
Long shoulder strap piece x 1 — 35½" (90cm) × ¾" (2cm)

Short shoulder strap piece x 1 — 13" (33cm) × ¾" (2cm)

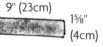
Inside rim leather pieces x 2 — 9" (23cm) × 1⅝" (4cm)

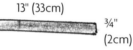
Strap tabs x 2 — 2⅜" (6cm) × ¾" (2cm)

Strap belt loops x 2 — 2⅜" (6cm) × ⅜" (1cm)

## Instructions

### 1

Sew the outside and inside of the flap pieces together with wrong sides facing and attach one piece of the buckle.

### 2

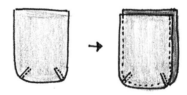

Cut slits in the corners of both main pieces of leather and sew the edges back together using a ⅛" (0.3cm) seam allowance. This creates darts in the corners, giving the bag more body. Then sew the front and back pieces together with right sides facing using a ¼" (0.5cm) allowance.

**3**

Turn right side out and fold the mouth of the bag down ⅜" (1cm).

**4**

Place the assembled flap onto the back of the bag body about ⅜" (1cm) down from the mouth and sew them together using two rows of stitches.

**5**

Next, attach the other piece of the buckle to the front of the bag body.

**6**

Open the bag and attach the strap tabs, with the metal loops threaded on, to either side of the body. Use glue to keep them positioned during stitching.

**7**

Sew the lining together using a ⅜"–½" (1–1.2cm) allowance. Do not turn right side out.

**8**

Place the lining into the body of the bag with wrong sides facing and sew them together using a ¼" (0.5cm) allowance. Remember to sew the lining with the flap open, or you may accidentally sew it onto the flap.

**9**

¼" (0.5cm)

Make one leather shoulder strap belt loop using rivets.

**10**

1¼" (3cm)

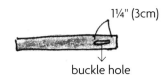

buckle hole

For the buckle end of the short shoulder strap, cut a small hole in the end of the strap for the buckle prong as shown.

**11**

Slide the leather loop made in step 9 onto the short shoulder strap, and add the buckle. Fold the end of the strap back past the loop and secure using a rivet. For extra hold, add a second strap belt loop as shown. The short strap is done!

**12**

For the long part of the shoulder strap, measure to your own height and punch as many buckle holes as desired.

**13**

Finally, string the ends of the straps without the buckle or holes through the metal loops on either side of the body of the bag and use rivets to fasten in place. You're done!

# Good Student Backpack

DIFFICULTY: ♥ ♥ ♥

See pattern side B

### Other materials
Rivets x 8
Large buckle x 1
Metal loops x 4
Back strap loops x 2

## Pieces and Supplies

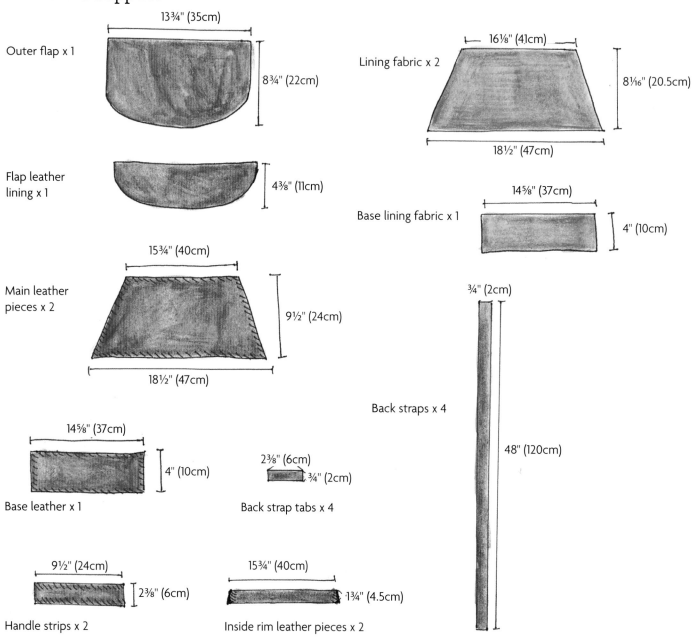

Outer flap x 1 — 13¾" (35cm) — 8¾" (22cm)

Flap leather lining x 1 — 4⅜" (11cm)

Main leather pieces x 2 — 15¾" (40cm) — 9½" (24cm) — 18½" (47cm)

Base leather x 1 — 14⅝" (37cm) — 4" (10cm)

Handle strips x 2 — 9½" (24cm) — 2⅜" (6cm)

Back strap tabs x 4 — 2⅜" (6cm) — ¾" (2cm)

Inside rim leather pieces x 2 — 15¾" (40cm) — 1¾" (4.5cm)

Lining fabric x 2 — 16⅛" (41cm) — 8¹/₁₆" (20.5cm) — 18½" (47cm)

Base lining fabric x 1 — 14⅝" (37cm) — 4" (10cm)

Back straps x 4 — ¾" (2cm) — 48" (120cm)

# Instructions

**1**

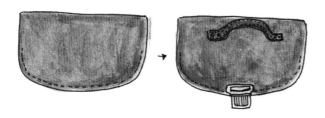

First sew the front and lining of the flap together with wrong sides facing, then sew on the handle and attach half of the flap buckle. For instructions, refer to Red Leather Executive Briefcase, page 106.

**2**

Glue the strap piecess together in two pairs and sew each pair together along the long edges using a ⅛" (0.3cm) seam allowance.

**3**

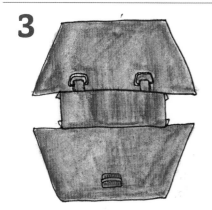

Next, stitch the bag base and the front side of the bag body together, placing the back strap tabs between the two pieces. Also sew the back side to the base and attach the other half of the front buckle to the front center of the bag.

**4**

Fold the mouth of the bag down about ⅜" (1cm) and position the back strap tabs on the back mouth of the body.

**5**

The top two seam allowances are ¾" (2cm); if they are too thick, they can be trimmed.

Place the lining into the body of the bag.

**6**

10" (25.5cm)

10" (25.5cm)

After sewing the lining into the body, sew on the flap about ¼" (0.5cm) down from the mouth of the bag.

**7**

Finally, string the straps though the loops and secure with rivets.

**8**

You're done!

# Red Executive Briefcase

DIFFICULTY: ♥♥♥♥

See pattern side B

## Pieces and Supplies

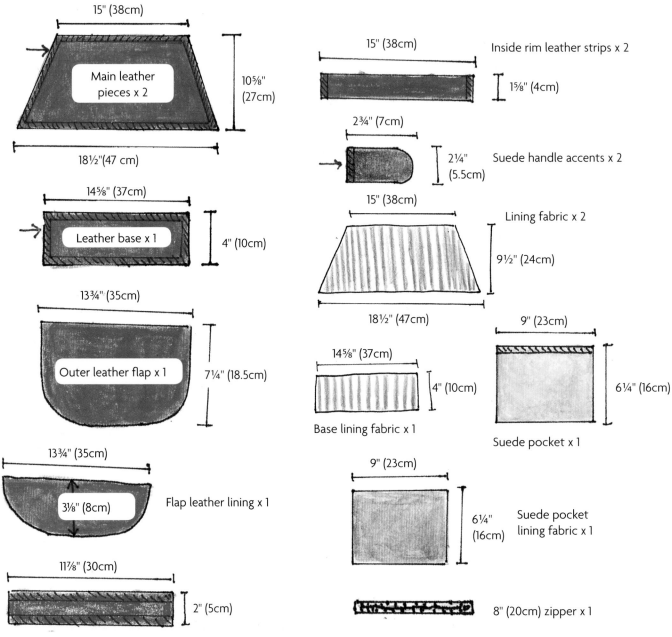

Thin the edges

15" (38cm)

Main leather pieces x 2

10⅝" (27cm)

18½" (47 cm)

14⅝" (37cm)

Leather base x 1

4" (10cm)

13¾" (35cm)

Outer leather flap x 1

7¼" (18.5cm)

13¾" (35cm)

3⅛" (8cm)

Flap leather lining x 1

11⅞" (30cm)

2" (5cm)

Leather handle strips x 2

15" (38cm)

Inside rim leather strips x 2

1⅝" (4cm)

2¾" (7cm)

2¼" (5.5cm)

Suede handle accents x 2

15" (38cm)

Lining fabric x 2

9½" (24cm)

18½" (47cm)

14⅝" (37cm)

4" (10cm)

Base lining fabric x 1

9" (23cm)

6¼" (16cm)

Suede pocket x 1

9" (23cm)

6¼" (16cm)

Suede pocket lining fabric x 1

8" (20cm) zipper x 1

106

# Instructions

**1**

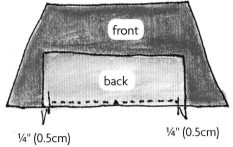

¼" (0.5cm)    ¼" (0.5cm)

Sew the leather base face down onto the front side of one main leather piece. Leave a ¼" (0.5cm) space on either side of the base.

**2**

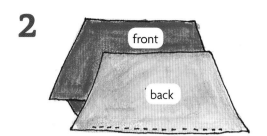

Next, using the same method, sew on the other main leather piece front side down.

**3**

Next, sew the front and back pieces together.

**4**

Then, sew the base and the front and back pieces together.

**5**

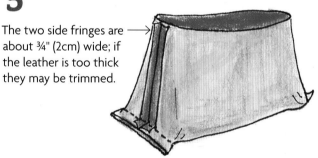

The two side fringes are about ¾" (2cm) wide; if the leather is too thick they may be trimmed.

Sew the other corner together using the same method.

**6**

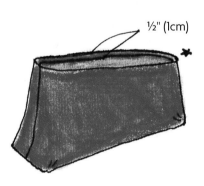

½" (1cm)

When the outside of the bag is all stitched together, turn the whole piece right side out, fold the top edges down about ⅜" (1cm), and glue them down with leather adhesive.

**7**

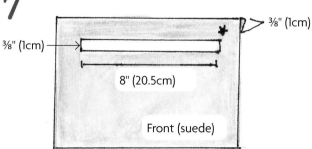

⅜" (1cm)    ⅜" (1cm)

8" (20.5cm)

Front (suede)

Make an 8" x ½" (20.5 x 1cm) cut for the zipper in the suede pocket and fold the top of the pocket down about ½" (1cm).

**8**

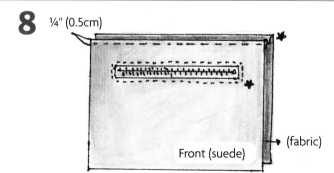

¼" (0.5cm)

Front (suede)    (fabric)

After sewing the zipper onto the suede, fold the top of the fabric pocket down ⅜" (1cm) and sew it onto the suede pocket, using a ¼" (0.5cm) seam allowance.

## 9

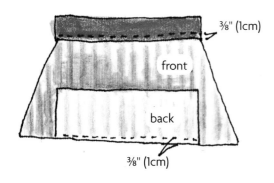

⅜" (1cm)

front

back

⅜" (1cm)

Sew one main fabric lining piece to the base fabric lining using the same method as the leather pieces, but add a leather lining strip at the top. Add a leather strip to the other fabric lining piece as well.

When you're done, sew the pocket onto one of the pieces of lining.

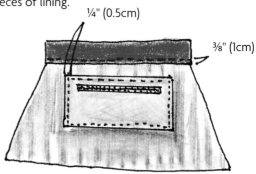

¼" (0.5cm)

⅜" (1cm)

## 10

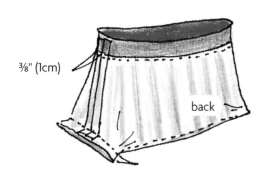

⅜" (1cm)

back

Then, sew the lining pieces together with a seam allowance of about ⅜" (1cm). After sewing the lining, there's no need to turn it right side out.

## 11

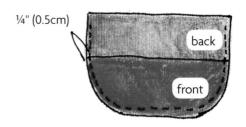

¼" (0.5cm)

back

front

Next, sew the outer and inner panels of the leather flap together.

## 12

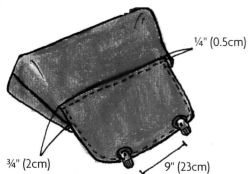

¼" (0.5cm)

¾" (2cm)

9" (23cm)

Then sew the flap onto the body of the bag, back tacking at the beginning and end of the seam for extra security. After the flap is sewn on, attach the tops of the buckles.

## 13

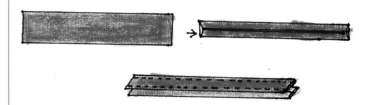

Fold the edges of the leather handle strips under about 1" (2.5cm), glue them down with leather adhesive, and sew them together.

## 14

After sewing the handle together, use rivets to connect the handle to the top of the flap.

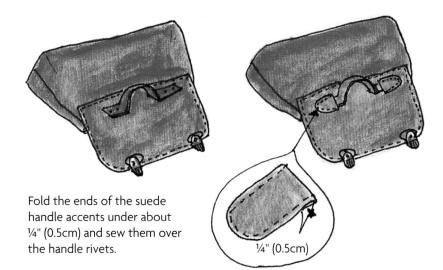

Fold the ends of the suede handle accents under about ¼" (0.5cm) and sew them over the handle rivets.

¼" (0.5cm)

## 15

After you attach the bottom of the buckles, the body of the briefcase is finished!

## 16

Take your already finished lining and place it directly into the body of the briefcase.

## 17

¼" (0.5cm)

Then, using a ¼" (0.5cm) seam allowance, stitch the lining to the body at the mouth of the bag.

## 18

Your briefcase is complete!

# Monogram Key Sleeves

DIFFICULTY: ♥

## Pieces and Supplies

### My house keys

## Instructions

### 1

First, measure your keys. Keys come in many different sizes, so remember to give them a little room!

### 2

Be sure to take notice of where the holes are, as each key differs from the next.

### 3

After punching the holes in the key sleeves, sew the edges together.

### 4

Take notice of the shapes of your keys to make the perfect sleeves for them!

# Index

**Note:** Page numbers in *italics* indicate projects.

**Sewing Stylish
Handbags & Totes**
ISBN 978-1-57421-422-2  **$22.99**
DO5393

**Sew Me! Sewing Basics**
ISBN 978-1-57421-423-9  **$19.99**
DO5394

**Sew Me! Sewing Home Decor**
ISBN 978-1-57421-504-5  **$14.99**
DO5425

**Sewing Leather Accessories**
ISBN 978-1-57421-623-3  **$14.99**
DO5313

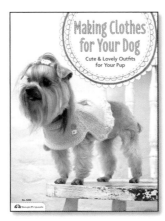

**Making Clothes for Your Dog**
ISBN 978-1-57421-610-3  **$24.99**
DO5300

**Pyrography Basics**
ISBN 978-1-57421-505-2  **$9.99**
DO5426

**Sewing Pretty Little Things**
ISBN 978-1-57421-611-0  **$19.99**
DO5301

**Five-Minute Quilt Blocks**
ISBN 978-1-57421-420-8  **$18.99**
DO5391

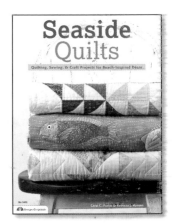

**Seaside Quilts**
ISBN 978-1-57421-431-4  **$24.99**
DO5402